THE CATCH CLUB
or
MERRY COMPANIONS

Part 2

Da Capo Press
Music Titles

Frederick Freedman
General Editor
University of California
at Los Angeles

THE CATCH CLUB

or

MERRY COMPANIONS

being A Choice Collection
of the Most Diverting Catches
for Three and Four Voices

Part 2

With an introduction to the Da Capo Edition by
Joel Newman
Columbia University

Da Capo Press
New York
1965

A
§ Da Capo Press®
Reprint Edition

Library of Congress Catalog Card Number 65-18504

© 1965 Da Capo Press
A Division of Consultants Bureau Enterprises, Inc.
227 West 17th Street • New York, N. Y. 10011

Printed in the United States of America

Note

A foreword to the Da Capo edition and indexes of composers, poets, titles, first lines, and number of voices required will be found in Part 1.

THE CATCH CLUB
or
MERRY COMPANIONS

Part 2

The Second Book of the
CATCH CLUB
or
Merry Companions

being

a Choice Collection of the most Diverting

CATCHES

for Three and Four Voices
Compos'd by the late

Mr. Henry Purcell   Dr. Blow &c.

2.ᵈ part.   price 2.ˢ 6.ᵈ

Nº 298

London. Printed for and Sold by I. Walsh Musick Printer and Instrument maker to his Majesty at the Harp & Hoboy in Catherine Street in the Strand.

An Alphabetical Table of the Catches contain'd in this Book

(1)

1 A. 3. Voc.   A Catch the words by Mr. Otway.   Mr. H. Purcell.

Would you know how we meet. o'er our Jolly full Bowls. as we mingle our

Liquors. we mingle our Souls. the sweet melts the sharp. the kind sooths the Strong.

and nothing but Friendship grows all the night long. we drink. laugh. and gra_tifie

ev_ry desire. Love. on_ly remains our unquenchable Fire.

2 A. 3. Voc.   Advice to Friend Jacob in Cornhill. writ and Set by Mr. Brown.

Come good sober Jacob. t'other quart. t'other quart. and no more, we know thou af-

fects neither drunkard. nor whore. yet methinks a good Fellow. for once. for once may be free.

with a Cup of this Creature. to our Friends. thee. and me. to en_li_ven the Spirit is to moisten. to

moisten thy clay. of which give 'em proof. at Bull and Mouth next first day.

way you silly Daughter, 'tis eve_ry She's concern, and if you won't believe me, look here.

look here, here, look here, here, look here, look here, here and you may learn: then taking her a-

side, she made the matter plain, O..........h mother, you're ten times worse! Oh you're

ten times worse! you're ten times worse! you're ten times worse! why sure you rid up _on the Main!

5 *A. 4. Voc.*   **A Catch.**

The silver Swan, who living had no Note, till Death approach'd unlock'd her silent

throat, leaning her breast against the Reedy shore, thus sung her first and last, and sung no

more, farewell all joys: Oh Death come close my eyes, more Geese than Swans now

live, more Fools than wise.

6 A. 3. Voc. The Agreement. (41). writ and Set by Mr. R. Brown.

All we here, whose names Sir, you find underwritten, do promise to pay unto

Benjamin Siffen, the sum of four Pounds for a part of a Room, he takes for con-

venience when marriage comes on, so witness our hands all, to what here is said man,

Sam Day, Harry Wils-n, and honest John Dedman.

7 A 3 Voc. Catch on good Claret. Set by Mr. George Day Organist of Winbourn in Dorsetshire.

Come drink a-bout Tom, let it pass about quicker, why the P-x dost thou Preach thus

over thy Liquor, one hour or two boys let us follow our drinking, away with such

Sots as will always be thinking, our brains will endure it, our pockets will bear it, come

drink about Tom, it is very good Claret.

8 *A.3.Voc.* — A Catch. (5) — Mr. H. Purcell.

Soldier, Soldier, take off thy Wine, and shake thy locks, and shake thy locks as I shake mine: how can I my poor locks shake, that have but Ten, I have but Ten Haires on my Pate, and one of them must go for Tythes, so there remains, so there remains but Four and Five, Four and Five, and that makes Nine, then take off your drink, then take off your drink as I take mine.

9 *A.3.Voc.* — A Catch. — Mr. H. Purcell.

Drink on, drink on, drink on, till Night be spent, and Sun do shine, did not the Gods give anxious Mortals Wine, to wash all Care, to wash all Care and Trouble from the heart? why then so soon, why then so soon shou'd Jo-vial Fellows part? come let this Bumper, let this Bumper for the next make way, who's sure to live, who's sure to live, and drink another day.

English-men fight, fight, fight, fight, fight, fight, fight to be sure the French run; Rash Tallards sur-

priz'd, surpriz'd to behold us so near, Bavaria's old Courage is sunk, is sunk in despair, Lead

on the Attack, then our Friends shall come after, we'll en-liven their Spirits, we'll en-liven their

Spirits, their Spirits, by our Enemies slaughter, 'tis for you brave Allies, 'tis for you brave Allies this great

march we took on us, fall back no-ble Germans' and only on-ly look on us, we'll shew you how easy

the Conquest is made, three English Huzzahs, Huzzahs, Huzzahs strike y French-men all Dead.

12 A.4.Voc.   :S: The King's Health.   Dr. Blow.

God preserve his Majesty, and for ever send him Victory, and confound all his Enemies.

Repeat Amen all the while this Catch is Singing, resting four Crotchets.

take off your Hock, Sir.   Amen.

15 A 3 Voc.   A Catch.   Mr. H. Purcell.

Bring the Bowl, and cool Nantz, bring the Bowl, and cool Nantz, and let us be mixing, we've a

great deal of buſneſs, we've a great deal of buſneſs, 'tis time to be fixing; dip, dip your diſh fair,

a..round to all jol...ly, jol-ly Punch drinkers, we looſe not a mi..nute, we looſe not a mi..nute

while we are our own ſhinkers: we need no damn'd drawers, our mo.........tions, our motions are

quicker, we ſit at the well boys, we ſit at the well boys, and drink richer Liquor.

16 A 4. Voc.   A Catch.   Mr. H. Purcell.

Pale Faces ſtand by, and our bright ones adore, we look like our Wine, you, worſe than our

Score, come light up our Pimples, all art we outſhine, when the plump God does paint, each ſtreak is di-

vine; Clean Glaſſes are Pencils, old Claret is Oyl, he that ſits for his Picture, muſt ſit a good while.

19 A 3 Voc.   The London Conſtable.   Mr. Henry Purcell.

Who comes there, ſtand, who comes there, ſtand, and came before the Conſtable, we'll know what you

are: what makes you out ſo late, ſays the midnight Magiſtrate, with a noddle full of Ale, in a wooden chair of

State: whence come you Sir, and whither do you go, you may be, Sir, a Jeſuit for ought I know, you may as

well Sir take me for a Mahometan. he ſpeaks Latin, ſecure him, he's a dangerous Man: to tell you the

truth Sir, I am an honeſt Tory. but here's a Crown to drink and there's an end of the Story. Good

Morrow Sir a civil Man is always welcome. go Barnaby Bounce, light the Gentleman home.

20 A 4. Voc.   A Saturday Night's Catch.   Mr. R. Brown.

Let's drink to all our wives, good health, and merry lives, but who to pleaſe them

cares, muſt live old Neſtor's years.

21 *A. 3. Voc.*   (12) A Catch.   Mr. H. Purcell.

True English men drink a good health to the Miter, let our Church ever Flourish,

tho' her Enemies spight her, may their cunning and For...ces, no longer prevail, but their

malice, as well as their Arguments, fail: Then re-member the Seven, who Supported our

Cause, as stout as our Martyrs, and as just as our Laws.

22 *A. 3. Voc.*   A Catch.   Mr. H. Purcell.

Sir Walter, enjoying his Damsel one night, He tickl'd and pleas'd her to so great a

height: that she cou'd not contain t'wards the end of the matter, but in Rapture cry'd out, O

sweet Sir Walter, O sweet Sir Walter, O sweet Sir Walter, O sweet Sir, sweet Sir Walter, O

switter swatter switter swatter switter swatter switter swatter switter swatter. Sir.

23 A.3.Voc. A Catch. Mr. H. Purcell.

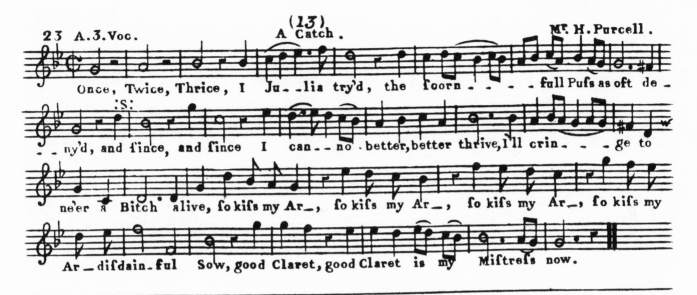

Once, Twice, Thrice, I Ju_lia try'd, the foorn_ _ _full Pufs as oft de_

ny'd, and fince, and fince I can _no better, better thrive, I'll crin_ _ _ge to

ne'er a Bitch alive, fo kifs my Ar_, fo kifs my Ar_, fo kifs my Ar_, fo kifs my

Ar _difdain_ful Sow, good Claret, good Claret is my Miftrefs now.

24 A.3.Voc. A Catch.

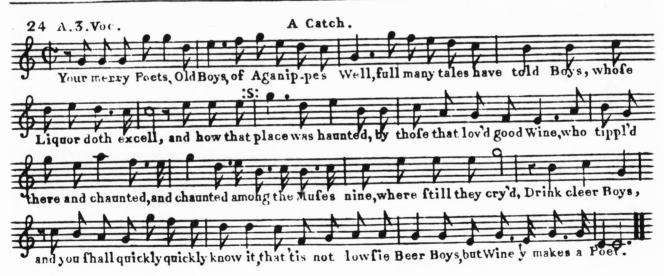

Your merry Poets, Old Boys, of Aganip_pes Well, full many tales have told Boys, whofe

Liquor doth excell, and how that place was haunted, by thofe that lov'd good Wine, who tippl'd

there and chaunted, and chaunted among the Mufes nine, where ftill they cry'd, Drink cleer Boys,

and you fhall quickly quickly know it, that 'tis not lowfie Beer Boys, but Wine y makes a Poet.

25 *A. 3. Voc.*   In Praiſe of the Punch Bowl.   Dr. Iohn Blow.

How ſhall we ſpeak thy praiſe, delicious Bowl, thou chear'ſt the Heart, and thou inſpir'ſt

the Soul; not Jove of Necter ſo Divine can boaſt, Ambro-ſia is inſiped to thy Toaſt:

Drink here, you ſons of wit, and you will own, the Punch Bowl is the on-ly Helicon.

26 *A. 3. Voc.*   A Catch.

Here lies a Woman who can deny it? She dy'd in peace, though liv'd un-

quiet. Her Huſband prays, if o're her grave you walk, you would tread ſoft,

you would tread ſoft: for if ſhe wake, for if ſhe wake ſhe'l talk; tread ſoft:

for if ſhe wake. ſhe'l talk.

29 A. 3. Voc. Celia Learning on the Spinnet. Mr. Iohn Isum.

When Cælia was Learning on the Spinnet to play, her Tutor stood by her to show her,

to show her. to show her, to show her the way; she shook not the'Note, which

angred him much. and made him, and made him cry Zounds 'tis a long prick. a long prick, a

long prick'd Note you touch: Surpriz'd was the Lady to hear him complain: and said. and

said, and said. I will shake it. I will shake it when I come to't again.

30 A. 3. Voc. A Catch. Mr. H. Purcell.

If:s. all be true that I do think. there are Five Reasons, there are Five Reasons we shou'd

Drink; good Wine. a Friend. or being Dry. or least we should be by and by; or any

other Reason. or any other Reason. or any other Reason. why. any Reason why.

31 A. 3. Voc.   A Catch on the London Watermen.   Mr. Barth. Isaac.

Will you go by water, Sir? I'm the next Sculler: go with my Fair up westward, Sir, my

Boat shall be no fuller: next oars, Sir, next oars; whither is't you go? to Fox-Hall or Westminster, or

through-Bridge hoa? pray master trim the Boat, and sit a little higher, you have a handsome Woman

by you, methinks you might sit nigher! come boy, lay the stretcher, and sit down to y oar, you sir! will you

change a Rogue for a Whore? you Sculler! look before you, with a-pox t'ye hold water: look!

look! the Rogue runs foul of us, remember this hereafter: come land us here at Kings Bridge,

aye Sir, if you're willing: here waterman there's six pence: good faith, 'tis worth a shilling.

32 A. 3. Voc. **The King of SPAIN'S Health.** *The words and musick by*
Mr. Henry Hall Organist of Heriford.

Come take off your Liquor, fill, fill it a-bout, that Flask of true Florence is hardly half out; the

Falcon it self of no better can boast, 'tis in a good hand, Sir, 'tis in a good hand Sir, and your

turn to Toast: The Queen, and the Prince are already gone round, the Churches well

willers, and noble Or...mond, with each worthy Member which was for the Bill, then

what shall I drink, then what shall I drink, or to whom shall I fill: Drink a

Health to the Hero which measures the Main, drink a Health to the new King, and true

King of Spain, and while Fortune smiles on us, and Eurus is kind, with re-

sounding Huz..zahs-------------- we'll add to the wind.

33 A. 3. Voc.   A Catch upon our Victory at Sea.   Dr. John Blow.

I know Brother Tar, I know Brother Tar, those French durst not stand us; nor the Dastardly Irish once venture to land us; if we Bang not such scoundrels may a stor............m ri.........se and strand us. But the Boson's shrill whistle cryes all, all, all, all hands a-loft Boys, and a Boat full of Punch is a rich mornings draught Boys; now tope we catt Harpin, now tope we catt Harpin, and then fore and aft Boys, Brother Bluff, Brother Bluff, 'tis a Gallon, 'tis a Gallon that now, now, now, now is a sinking, to our Landmen who never yet knew what was shrinking, we'll cover our Descent with Huzzas, Huzzas and dow................n drinking.

36 A. 4. Voc.   A Catch on Tobacco   Sung by 4 Men while smoaking their Pipes.

Good, good indeed, the Herb's good weed, fill thy Pipe Will, and I prithee Sam fill, for

sure we may smoak, and yet sing still, and yet sing still, what say the Learned, what say the

Learned, Vita fumus, Vita fumus, 'tis what you, and I, and he, and I, you and he

and I, and all of us, Sumus, But then to the Learned say we again, if life's a smoak as

they maintain, if life's a Vapour, without doubt, when a Man does dye, they shou'd not

cry, that his Glass is run, but his Pipe is out; But whether we smoak, or whether we sing, let's be

Loyal, and remember the King, let him live, and let his Foes vanish, thus, thus, thus, like,

like a Pipe, like a Pipe of Spanish, thus, thus, like a Pipe of Spanish.

37 A.3.Voc. A Catch on S.r John and his Lady Set by Mr. R. Brown.

Said S.r John to his Lady, as kissing, as kissing they sate, shall we now go to dinner, or to you know,

to you know what. with a Languishing look, reply'd, reply'd the good Lady, S.r John what you

please for your dinner. your dinner's not ready, but sweet good S.r John, S.r John, be'nt thus given to

wallow. if you stir but up stairs, I protest, I protest I must follow.

38 A.3.Voc. A Catch. by M.r R. Brown.

Hiccop

Was ever Mortal Man so fitted. so fitted. the Master Drunk. the Master Drunk

the Master Drunk. and horse. and horse Committed. the Master Drunk. and horse, and

horse Committed. but horse for thy self take thou no care. thou will be a horse, will be a

horse when he, when he's no Mayor.

39 A.3. Voc.   A. Catch.   Mr. H. Purcell.

Come come let us Drink, let us Drink, let us Drink, let us Drink, 'tis in vain to

think, like Fools on Grief or sadness, let our Money fly, and our Sorrows die, all

worldly Care is Madness, but Wine, Wine, Wine, Wine, Wine and good cheer, will in spight of our

fear, in spire — — our Hearts with Mirth Boys, the time we live, to Wine, to Wine let us give, since

all, since all must turn to Earth Boys, hand, hand about, hand, hand about, hand hand about, the

Bowl, the delight of my Soul, and to my Hand, to my Hand commend it, a Fig, a Fig for

Chink, 'twas made to buy Drink and before — — we go hence we'll spend it.

40 A.3. Voc. A Catch.

Have you obferv'd the Wench in the ftreet, fhe's fcarce any Hofe or Shooes to her Feet, yet

fhe is very merry, and when fhe cries, fhe Sings I ha Hot Codlins, Hot Codlins,

or have you ever feen, or heard the Mortal with a Lion taw_ny Beard, he

lives as merrily as any heart can wifh and ftill he cries Buy a Brifh, Buy a Brifh,

Since thefe are merry why fhould we take care, Mu_ficians like Ca_melians muft

live by the Air, Then let's be blith and bonny, and no good Meeting balk, for

when we have no money, we fhall find Chalk.

45 A. 3. Voc.　　　　　A Catch.　　　(28)　　　　Mr. John Eccles.

Confusion, confusion to the pow'r.... of Cupid: brisk Wine, brisk Wine ne'er

made a Mortal stupid:　Drink, drink,　drink, drink, while sober sots look

pale, condemn'd to Claps, condemn'd to Claps and foggy Ale.　a pox of Love, a

pox of Love, there's nothing in it, a Bumper gives the happy, happy minute.

46 A. 3. Voc.　　A Catch on the famous Expedition at Vigo by Mr. R. Brown.

O're Neptune's Dominions brave Ormond sail'd home, from fright'ning Jack

Spaniard with Cales heavy Doom; But Jack he has trick'd thee, be-stir thy old

Bones, and hasten to Vigo to save thy Galloons, Marbleu crys the Monsieur, Jack

curses his Fate, and swears he'll trust French-men no more with his Plate.

(47) A. 3. Voc.   (29)   A Catch.   Mr. H. Purcell

'Tis too late for a Coach, and too soon to reel home, we have freedom to stagger when the

Town is our own: let's whirle it away, and whip Six-pen-ces round, till the Drawers are

founder'd, and the Hogshead does sound: The Glass stays with you, Tom, save your Tide,

pull a-way, one minute of Mid-night is worth a whole Day.

(48) A. 3. Voc.   A Catch.

Come hither Tom and make up three, and sing this Catch with me; though the Tune be old, I

dare be bold, 'tis good if we all agree: So now comes in my noble Jack, keep Time upon his back:

If he miss I do swear, I'll pull him by the ear, un til I do hear it crack. Now listen to the Bass, for

he will us disgrace; I fear the Lout will first be out, he makes such an ugly face.

(49) A.3.Voc.

A Catch Upon Port Wine.

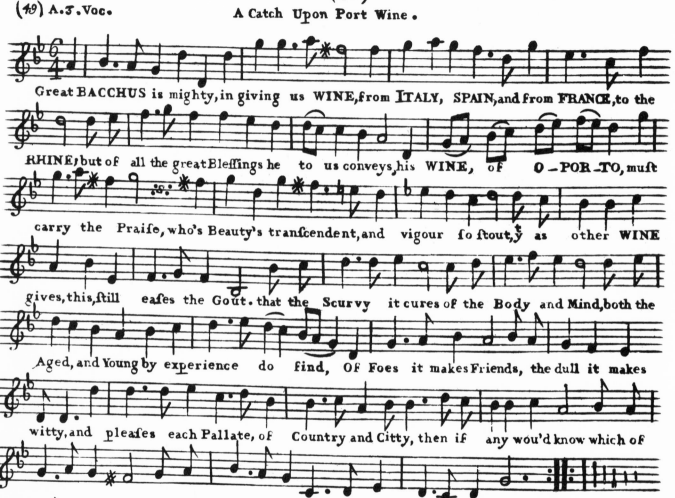

Great BACCHUS is mighty, in giving us WINE, from ITALY, SPAIN, and from FRANCE, to the

RHINE, but of all the great Bleffings he to us conveys, his WINE, of O—POR—TO, muft

carry the Praife, who's Beauty's tranfcendent, and vigour fo ftout, y as other WINE

gives, this, ftill eafes the Gout. that the Scurvy it cures of the Body and Mind, both the

Aged, and Young by experience do find, Of Foes it makes Friends, the dull it makes

witty, and pleafes each Pallate, of Country and Citty, then if any wou'd know which of

WINE'S the beft fort, let him take for his an-fwer, A Bottle of PORT.

(50)A. 3. Voc.

A Catch.

If any so wise is, that Sack he despises, let him drink his Small Beer and be Sober, whilst we drink Sack and sing, as if it were Spring, he shall droop like the Trees in Oc-to-ber, But be sure over night, if this Dog do you bite, you take it henceforth for a warning, soon as out of your Bed, to set-tle your Head, take a hair of his tail in the morning: And be not so fil-ly, to fol-low old LILLY, for there's nothing but Sack y can tune us; let his NE-AS-SUESCAS be put in his Cap-case, and sing BI-BI-TO- VI-NUM JEJU-NUS.

(51) A Catch on the Modern Courage and Conduct of the French. Set by Mr. Rich.d Brown.

Ah sorry poor French-men, I grieve at your Fates, your Armies are beaten, your cunning abates; In Field nor in Town, dare you stand your own Ground. what dismall effects after this will be found; At Audenards Battle, that may nt be forgot, you Ran from your Comrade half dead on the spot. Liie's Fortress no less must with shame be remember'd. the Siege was push'd close and you tamely surrender'd. the Sons of the Blood. by Example Mr. Prouis, can't animate wretches more dull than a Cow is. for shame then go home to your Sallads and Pottage, resign your fine Towns, suck your paws in a Cottage.

52 A. 3. Voc.   A Catch.   Mr. H. Purcell.

Sum up all the delights, sum up all, all, sum up all the delights the world does produce, the

darling allurements now chiefly in use, you'll find when compar'd, there's none can con‿

tend, with the solid enjoyments of Bottle, and Friend, for Honour, or wealth,

or Beauty may waste, those Joys often fade, but rarely do last, they're so hard to at‿

tain, and so easily lost, that the Pleasure ne'er answers the trouble and cost, none like

wine, none like wine and true friendship are lasting and sure, from Jealousie free,

and from envy secure, then fill up the Glasses untill they run o'er, a Friend and good

Wine are the charms we adore.

55 *A. 3. Voc.*   The King's Health.   Mr. Jeremy Clarke

Here's a Health to the King, who has said from the Throne, that His Heart is true

English as well as our own: that His Heart is true English, His Heart is true English, as

well as our own: And the Church fix't by Law is resolv'd to maintain; thro' the course of His

Life and the course of His Reign; thro' the course of His Life, thro the course of His Life,

and the course of His Reign: Thus we need not to fear any danger to come, while our

Arms Rule abroad, and our King Reigns at home; while our Arms Rule abroad, while our

Arms Rule abroad, and our King Reigns at home.

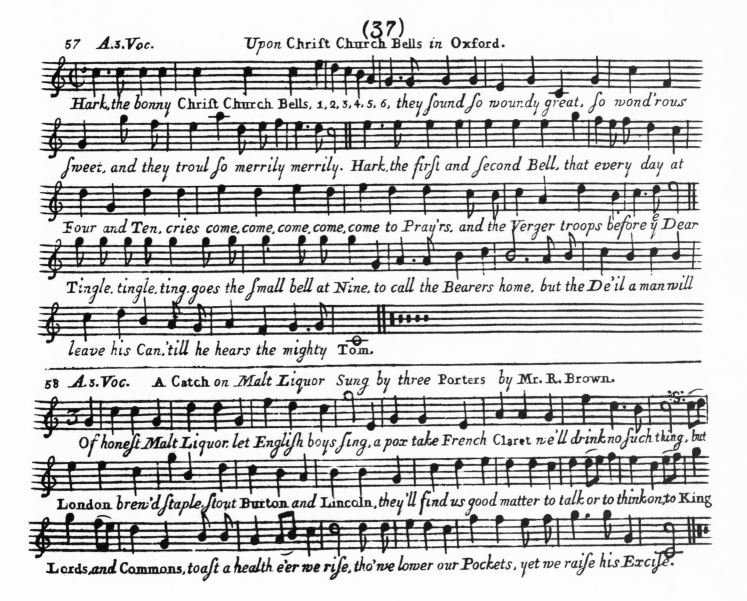

57 *A.*3.*Voc.*   Upon Chrift Church Bells *in* Oxford.

Hark, the bonny Chrift Church Bells, 1, 2, 3, 4, 5, 6, they found fo woundy great, fo wond'rous

fweet, and they troul fo merrily merrily. Hark, the firft and fecond Bell, that every day at

Four and Ten, cries come, come, come, come, come to Pray'rs, and the Verger troops before y̌ Dear

Tingle, tingle, ting, goes the fmall bell at Nine, to call the Bearers home, but the De'il a man will

leave his Can, till he hears the mighty Tom.

58 *A.*3.*Voc.*   A Catch *on* Malt Liquor Sung *by* three Porters   *by* Mr. R. Brown.

Of honeft Malt Liquor, let Englifh boys fing, a pox take French Claret we'll drink no fuch thing, but

London bren'd ftaple, ftout Burton and Lincoln, they'll find us good matter to talk or to think on, to King

Lords, and Commons, toaft a health e'er we rife, tho'we lower our Pockets, yet we raife his Excife.

59 A. 3. Voc.   A (38) Catch.   Mr. Willis.

Here Tom, here's a Health. Here Tom, here's a Health, here's a Health, which re-
fu............je if you dare; Fill up his Glaſs, fill it up, fill it up, fill up his Glaſs, fill, fill it
up, and let him drink, let him dri......nk, drink, drink fair to the beſt of our Friends, to the beſt, to the
beſt, to the beſt of our Friends, and the leaſt of our Care, and the leaſt of our Care.

Through Baſs to the Catch.

60   (A Catch to a Minuet. Mr. Tho. Ridd.)   Mr. Williams.

Let's fuddle our Noſes Tom and be merry, with a Glaſs of good ſtrength'ning Sherry; and never
plot, plot more, but of Wine to get ſtore; ſince we ſee that we always miſcarry: Rich Bumpers
on us no miſcheif will bring, but Plotting will ſend's to Hell in a String.

61 *A.* 4. *Voc.*   Second Part of Bartholomew Fair.   Dr. Blow.

:S: Here are the Rarities of the whole Fair, Pimperle-Pimp, and the wise Dancing Mare; here's

valiant St. George and the Dragon, a Farce, a Girl of Fifteen with strange moles on her Ar —

Here is Vi-en-na besieg'd, a rare thing, and here's Punchinel-lo, shown thrice to the King. Ladies

mask'd to the Cloysters re-pair; but there will be no Raffling, a Pox take the Mayor.

62 *A.* 3. *Voc.*   A Catch.   Mr. Willis.

Frank, what shall we do, for an Hour or two, this Sr. Sol in a Morning moves damnable slow,

yet at night with a Pox, he's always in haste, you may swear his Road's down hill by his driving so

fast, ne'er mind the old Fool, he's still going astray, once Drunken Dick Phaeton hit of the way.

Through Bass
to the Catch.

63 A 3. Voc.   A Catch.   Mr. Morgan.

Quoth Jack on a time, to Tom, I'll declare it, I've a mind we shou'd Fuddle our Noses with Claret.

Says Tom it will do you more harm than you think, fye on you says Jack who can live without drink

I'll ne'er balk my wine, here's to thy dispose, Tom pretends not to drink, pray look on his Nose.

54 A 3 Voc. Catch on a Parson's decriped old Dog call'd Barnet   by Mr. R. Brown.

'Tis pity poor Barnet, a Vigilant, Vigilant Curr. that us'd for to bark, if a mouse, if a

mouse, a mouse did but stir, should being grown old and unable, unable to bark, be

doom'd by a Priest, be doom'd by a Priest, to be hang'd by his Clark, I pray good Sir

therefore, weigh right well, right well his Case, and save us poor Barnet, hang

Cleric, hang Cleric, hang Cleric in s place.

67 A. 3. Voc.   A Catch.

Say good master Bacchus, a-stride on your Butt, since our Champagn's all gone, and our Claret's run out; which of all the brisk Wines in your Empire that grow, will serve to delight your poor Drunkards below? Resolve us, Grave Sir, and soon send it over, lest we dye, lest we dye of the Sin of be'ng Sober.

68 A. 3. Voc.   A Catch.

She that will eat her Breakfast in her Bed, and spend the morn in dressing of her head, and sit at dinner like a Maiden Bride, and nothing do all day but talk of Pride: Jove of his mercy may do much to save her, but what a case is he in that shall have her.

69 A. 3. Voc.   On a Widow who Married an old Widower.   :S:

Had she not Care enough, Care enough, had she not Care enough, Care enough of the old man: She

wed him, She fed him, and to the Bed she led him. for sev'n long winters she lifted him on: But

Oh! how she nigl'd him, nigl'd him, nigl'd him! Oh! how she nigl'd him all the Night long!

70 A. 3. Voc.   A Catch.

There was three Cooks in Colebrook, and they fell out with our Cook, and all was for a

Pudding he took and from the Cook of Colebrook: There was Swash Cook, and Slash Cook.   :S:

and thy Nose in my Narse Cook, and all was for a Pud-ding he took, and from the Cook of

Colebrook; they all fell upon our Cook, and mumbled him so that he did look as black as the

Pudding which that he took, and from the Cook of Colebrook.

(73) A. 3. Voc.   A Catch. (45)   Mr. Jeremy Clarke.

In Drinking full Bumpers there is no deceit. then let's not repine at our sitting up late; Come light all your Pipes. up. no Sun we do need. we can see what we Drink by the light of the Weed. may our Jolly Club ne'er by Intruders be broke. then our Sorrow in clouds shall ascend like our Smoak.

(74) A. 3. Voc.   A Catch.   Mr. H. Purcell.

An Ape, a Lyon, a Fox. and an Ass. do shew forth man's Life as it were in a Glass; for Apish we are till Twenty and one. and af-ter that. Ly-ons till Forty be gone: then witty as Foxes till Threescore and Ten, but after that Asses. and so no more Men.

A Dove, a Sparrow, a Parrot, a Crow,
As plainly sets forth how you Women may know:
Harmless they are. till Thirteen be gone.

Then Wanton as Sparrows till Forty draw on:
Then Prating as Parrots till Threescore be o're,
Then Birds of ill Omen. and Women no more.

(46)

A 3 Voc.   A Catch

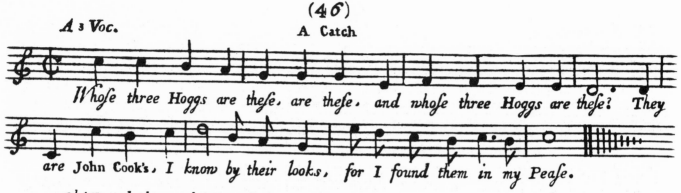

Whoſe three Hoggs are theſe, are theſe, and whoſe three Hoggs are theſe? They

are John Cook's, I know by their looks, for I found them in my Peaſe.

Oh! Pound them, oh! Pound them, but I dare not for my life.
For if I ſhou'd Pound John Cook's Hoggs, I ſhou'd never kiſs John Cook's Wife:
Cho: But as for John Cooks Wife, I'll ſay no more than mum,
Then here's to thee, thou firſt Hogg, untill the Second come.

Note: Theſe two lines are to be Sung thrice with theſe words at laſt. (I prithee man take him home)

(76) A 3 Voc.   A Catch.   Mr. H. Purcell.

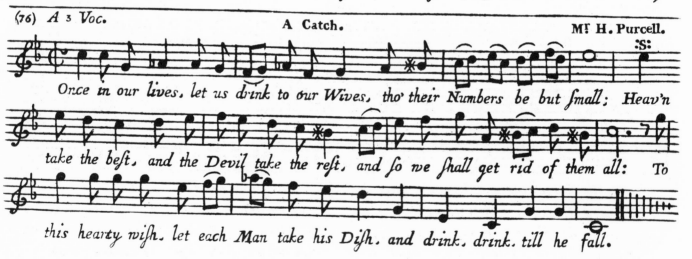

Once in our lives, let us drink to our Wives, tho' their Numbers be but ſmall: Heav'n

take the beſt, and the Devil take the reſt, and ſo we ſhall get rid of them all: To

this hearty wiſh, let each Man take his Diſh, and drink, drink, till he fall.

A 3 Voc.

A Catch.

Good Symon, how comes it your Nose looks so red. and your Cheeks and Lips look so

pale? Sure the heat of your Toast. your Nose did so roast. when they were both sous'd in

Ale: It shows like the spire of Paul's-Steeple on fire. each Ruby darts forth such

lightning flashes. while your face looks as dead. as if it were Lead. and cover'd all

o'er with Ashes. Now to heighten his colour. yet fill his pot. fill his pot fuller. and

nick it not so with froth: Cra-mercy mine Host. it shall save thee a Toast: Sup

Symon. for here is good Broth.